You Tell

"There are no easy immensely brilliant book, save that, as with other eccentric miniaturists—Walser or Dickinson or Davis—brevity of expression belies vastness of thought. A reflection on the seasons, a meditation on time, an autobiography filtered through art, *You Tell the Stories You Need to Believe* is finally—though there's nothing conventionally pious about it—a prayer, its devotion bent equally toward the luminous particulars of the world and the ever deferred, ever hoped-for gifts of the spirit. I loved it more than I can say."

—Garth Greenwell, author of *Cleanness*
and *What Belongs to You*

"Rebecca Brown is a companionable writer, totally honest, cultured in an unintimidating way, freely associating with total freedom and virtuoso associations."

—Edmund White, author of *A Boy's Own Story*
and *Genet: A Biography*

"Rebecca Brown's wonderful *You Tell the Stories You Need to Believe* is a deeply moving distillation of her life's awareness of struggle, and art, and loneliness growing up, and the redemptive power of love, all told in a style simpler and more direct than some of her earlier works, and yet very moving in its purity and honesty."

—Rachel Pollack, author of *Godmother Night* and
Unquenchable Fire

"A poet has found a new way to praise the seasons! In each time of year, with its promise or its feared return, its arrival somehow always new, its disillusions and startling fulfillments, its frightening, beautiful mirror in the seasons of human life, Rebecca Brown has found the shape of time itself and found it good."

—Valerie Trueblood, author of *Terrarium: New and Selected Stories* and *Search Party: Stories of Rescue*

PRAISE FOR REBECCA BROWN:

"Brown is a great writer... Every chapter... is beautifully composed, resonant, tough. It reads as dark but also true and moving... readable and untakeable at once."

—Ali Smith, *The Guardian* (UK)

"Ripe and imaginative, often funny, and sliding craftily between fact and wishful fantasy."

—*The Sunday Times* (London)

"A strange and wonderful first-person voice emerges from the stories of Rebecca Brown, who strips her language of convention to lay bare the ferocious rituals of love and need."

—*The New York Times Book Review*

You Tell the Stories
You Need to Believe

YOU TELL THE STORIES
YOU NEED TO BELIEVE

on the four seasons,
time and love, death and
growing up

Rebecca Brown

CHATWIN BOOKS

Cover design & illustration (based on *Adam & Eve*, by Jakob Rueff, *Francoforti ad Moenum*, 1580, via NLM Digital Collections) by Vladimir Verano

Book design by Annie Brulé

Author photograph by Phil Bevis

ISBN: 978-163398-134-8

CHATWIN BOOKS
www.ChatwinBooks.com

For Christopher Frizzelle

Contents

*

Spring

Spring

SPRING IS WHEN THE LIGHT starts coming back. Green things shoot out of the earth and the world unthaws and gets moist and soft and the wind stops whipping and turns into breezes and little girls get Easter dresses and shiny shoes and little boys dress up in short long pants and cute bow ties and everyone gets Easter baskets and finds bright colored eggs. People sweep away dead, stuck leaves and open the windows and throw away stuff. Mammals come out of their winter caves and start shedding pounds and layers and eating healthy. They turn to the sun and show their faces and sap starts to rise and everything's new again.

But it isn't like that for everyone.

Maybe, really, it isn't like that at all.

Everyone else seems happy and eager to start again but you are not, no, you don't want to start again, you don't want to go through another year. The winter was hard but it felt outside how you felt inside—the dark and gray became you. In winter you were not the only one who didn't want to get out of bed or leave the house or do things or remember. You didn't feel good, but at least you weren't out of seasonal sync. The outside looked like you inside.

Here's part of the start of T. S. Eliot's *The Waste Land,* from 1922:

> *Winter kept us warm, covering*
> *Earth in forgetful snow feeding*
> *A little life with dried tubers.*

A tuber is an underground stem or root. The word comes from Latin for "swollen."

We used to have a kids' book called *The Story of the Root Children,* which begins:

> *Under the ground, deep in the earth among the roots of the trees, the little root children were fast asleep all winter long. They didn't feel the biting wind, the cold snow, or the stinging hailstorms. They slept peacefully in their warm burrows...*

It's right they spend their tuber lives asleep.

Mother Earth wakes the root children up: "Time to get up now. You've slept long enough. Spring is coming and there's work to be done."

The root children go to work. They look alike and have bowl-cut hair and dress in plain brown smocks. In the rooty dirt beneath the ground they clean and paint the shells of beetles and roaches. Above them the land is golden and light. To get out of the underworld the children have to climb. They walk in a row up the root of a tree and when they get outside they meet a snail.

The Root Children was published in 1906 and the pictures are old-timey and the person who wrote and illustrated it was Sibylle von Olfers, aka Sister Maria Aloysia after she joined the Sisters of Saint Elizabeth, known as "The Gray Nuns," because they wore gray hoods with their plain brown habits. The Sisters worked with people too sick for hospitals—they went to their homes to care for them and, kindly, help them die. Sister Maria Aloysia died at 35. The root children crawling up from below look like souls coming up from the harrowing of hell.

Jesus went down to hell in spring. It was after he died and was laid in the tomb. He went down to harrow hell—and then he brought up the dead.

Persephone went to hell and came back too. Zeus, the father of gods, let Hades, god of the underworld, who was in love with Persephone, abduct her because Demeter, her mom, wouldn't let Persephone go out with a guy from hell. So Hades abducted—that is, he raped—Persephone. He took her to hell. While Demeter, the goddess of fertility and earth, looked for her, she turned the crops to crap and kept the plants from growing. After months of searching, she found Persephone in the underworld and brought her back. But because of a trick too complex to tell you here, Persephone has to go back to the underworld each year for a while, which is winter, then gets to come back above each year for a while, which is spring.

Spring is a time when your cover is blown. You get exposed and then bad things can happen.

What if sometime the girl did not come back? What if she wanted not to come back because she had gotten tired of going back and forth, of every year getting covered and then uncovered again, of living in two different worlds, the one where you're quiet and unseen in the dark, and then the other one? What if she couldn't bear it one more time?

Why do we need to believe she will come back?

Stravinsky's *The Rite of Spring* is also about a rape. The audience rioted when it premiered in 1913, not because of the rape, which was, as art so often likes to make it, "discreet," but because of Diaghilev's brutal dance. The story is about what's been in the dark then woken up, pent up and fevered, murderous. In *An Autobiography*, Stravinsky described the piece as having begun in "a fleeting vision," in which he saw a pagan rite where a young girl danced to death in front of a circle of elders, a sacrifice, they decided, to propitiate the god of spring.

Dear God, what kind of god would ask for that?

March was named for Mars, the god of war. In the olden days you didn't wage war in the winter because your soldiers and horses would freeze and you couldn't travel. You waited until the world began to thaw and you could travel and not freeze again and get back to your pillaging.

April may be named (people disagree) after the Latin *aperire*, "to open," as in buds, flowers, etc. But opening can be dangerous. Exposure can be scary to the unprotected self. April is the cruelest month (*The Waste Land*).

May may be named for Maia, a Roman goddess (not unlike the Greek Demeter) of plants and of fertility. And maybe also for *maiores*, the "elders" who were honored by Romans this time of the year.

Before or after they saw the poor girl dance herself to death?

The elders are the people who survive. They'll grieve and spend the rest of their lives remembering.

You want to say to them, "You're not alone." You want to say, "Don't be ashamed, you're not to blame." You want to say, "My heart is going out to you, your poor surviving soul."

Doctors call spring "the suicide season." Though everyone thinks the winter holidays depress the most (the pressures of family or not having one, the horrible false good cheer, shopping mall music), it's spring. Medical people first noticed this trend in the early 19th century. Recent studies have suggested that sunshine triggers suicidal thoughts, as do increases in temperature, the pollen count, barometric pressure, rain, the phases of the moon.

Spring Fever is either an increase in or a decrease of your energy. Your serotonin levels, which are affected by sunlight, are depleted in the winter. When the light comes back and more serotonin gets made in you, it can pep you up, or because of the work to produce it in you, exhaust you. These studies are all disputed, of course, and none of them, really, will tell the reason why. Whatever is going on in you or your body or world, one thing that's sure about spring is we've decided what it means—a new beginning, a fresh new start, a brand-new better you. But if everyone near you is hopeful and bright and you can't imagine your life could improve, you might feel awful or worse.

Whenever I hear the opening of "Spring," from Vivaldi's *The Four Seasons,* I want to scream. It's chipper. It's pert. It's a plastic smile. It's trying too hard to twinkle. In the second and third movements, you can hear what's still underneath, what couldn't be spring-cleaned away despite your trying: It's something forever sad.

There's a zillion translations of *The Canterbury Tales*. How's this for my amalgam:

> *When April with her showers sweet, has pierced the drought of March to the root, and bathed each vein with the powerful liquor that gives birth to flowers... that's when people want to go on pilgrimages... It was during this season that, one day, in Southwark, at the Tabard Pub, I lay...*

While plants outside are being soaked with life-giving rain, the narrator is lying down in a bar. People who lie down in bars are drunk. They're miserable; they love company:

> *There came at nightfall to that bar, twenty-nine or so different people who had started to chat and hang out together, pilgrims.*

Sometimes to get your mind away, you go out for a walk. Sometimes you walk and walk and walk. Sometimes when you do that with people you tell each other stories to pass the time.

You tell the stories you need to believe.

Sylvia Plath took her life in February, just before the start of spring. So did, more than 30 years later, the dramatist Sarah Kane. One recent winter it was Philip Seymour Hoffman. Maybe he didn't plan to die, but when is an overdose not the end of a long time of trying to die?

I don't remember what season it was in which Joe took his life. I try hard not to think of suicide. Most of that kind of stuff I have worked to forget. But I do remember him visiting me two weekends before and how we stayed up late and giggled and laughed and talked about who we liked but didn't like us. He slept on a futon on the floor, I slept on the bed beside it. He seemed really happy and I was glad—I felt relieved and was very glad for him. I also remember when they called and taking the bus back to town and all of us in the house crying and laughing and not knowing what but thinking had it been inevitable or was there something I should have seen? Then all of us at the grave site, sunny and shivering.

Spring is also a word for when someone escapes from prison. Sometimes they get help from friends outside, as in "They sprung him out." But sometimes the poor bastards have to escape alone.

May God have mercy upon their souls.

❋

Summer

Summer

WHEN SUMMER IS COMING you start to see ads for tanning booths and how to lose weight and get in shape so you'll look good in a bathing suit. By summer you need to be beautiful.

No wonder I don't like summer.

In the States it begins with remembering and death— Memorial Day. We're supposed to remember our soldiers who died in wars we sent them to kill in. I sort of think of this, but not very much. I have never lost anyone in a war and don't want the start of summer to bum me out. What I want is a day off work. I want someone to fix me barbecue and to eat homemade deviled eggs and pie. I want to drink gin and tonics and fall asleep in the sun and not wake up.

One summer I went to a cabin near the coast. I teach from the autumn to spring and I sometimes pretend that when summer comes, I'll get back to my own work and write. Sometimes I do, but it seems to get harder and harder. The summers get shorter and hotter and more and more I want to nap. My brain feels like soup.

In the cabin there was a mattress and toilet and hot plate and sink but the shower was at a place at the end of the parking lot. Outside, past the trees, kids played at the beach while their mothers and dads sat on chairs beneath umbrellas and slathered on suntan lotion. Teenagers got on boogie boards and some of them even surfed. They strutted around with their fit, tan, hairless bodies all glistening with oil. I stayed in my cabin away from them and dozed in and out of a big fat biography of a chubby eccentric writer. I liked being in a beautiful place and not getting out of bed to go be outside in it. I loved knowing people were all around but not having to talk or listen or be nice to anyone or pretend I was happy.

At night, after most of the day visitors had gone, I walked into town. There wasn't a restaurant or bar, just a bunch of smallish houses with satellite dishes and stuff in the yard and trucks. Sometimes people would look out their windows at me but nobody ever said anything including me.

Summer was different when I was a kid. The summer was like it was not even really real or not just a time but an actual place you could go. Where school and homework and parents and not knowing how to look never even happened.

Summer was riding bikes.

I rode my big brother's from when he was small, a giant clunky Schwinn. Lydia and Kenneth, who came after school got out to spend the summer with their dad, had cool bikes with banana seats and handlebars. Their father bought them new for them when he moved here with his new wife.

When they were here to visit him it was a different place. Nobody had to go to school and nobody acted like they didn't know you. In summer parents didn't yell as much because we were outside a lot, not inside, in their hair. If we were inside it was at Lydia and Kenneth's. Their dad and his new wife didn't yell but gave us Cokes or ice cream sandwiches or frozen Snickers bars. We rode around all day everywhere, to the park and the school and the college and church then past to the land outside the edge of town. One day we found a place behind a clump of trees where someone had cut the fence so you could crawl under. We got down on our bellies and crawled then somebody brought a wire cutter from their dad's and we cut the fence up to the top and bent the wires back so we could ride through.

It was dusty and dry and our legs and shorts and T-shirts got brown and scratched but nobody really noticed. The dirt got packed beneath where we rode, sometimes it even looked shiny. There were bushes and branches and nail-filled boards and crushed-up hole-filled cans. One time we found a mattress. The springs were popped-through the cover and ants were crawling on it. The trees were low to the ground with long loose stretched-out branches.

There were also many dogs. They were scrawny and some were frightening, with yellow teeth and scabs or places their fur was bit. We yelled at them and waved sticks and climbed trees to get away from them. We made a tree fort in one of the trees. The girls had stopped playing with dolls and with statues of horses and nobody played anymore with G.I. Joes or trucks. Crawford and Louis and Tammy and Tina, the twins, and Kenneth and Lydia and I worked on our fort then rode back to Kenneth and Lydia's. We then rode back with nails and ropes and a hammer. Some of the dogs kept being there and after a while, we petted them and brought them sandwiches.

One of the dogs started following me home but my mother would not allow the dog inside.

One of those summers, the song "The Door into Summer" came out, on *Pisces, Aquarius, Capricorn & Jones Ltd.*, the fourth album by the Monkees. Before we came back to the States, when we lived in Spain, there was mostly the Beatles and the Rolling Stones, but after we came back there was TV after school and the Monkees and Paul Revere and everyone telling you about astrology. You were supposed to be able to figure out secret things about yourself and planets such as who you were compatible with. I knew what my sign was, and I guessed I was kind of like it, but all of the signs, depending on how you thought about them or who was telling you, could kind of apply. I didn't believe in them but I was curious about who could be compatible with me. Could anyone? I tried to ask someone their sign one time, as if it were no big deal, but then I didn't know what to say next. I didn't know how to say anything or to stand in my skin

anymore. In summer you didn't see certain people—
only the people you didn't feel ugly around.

The summer was crabgrass beneath your feet. You
felt it on the sides of your flip-flops and sticky white
broken stems of ripened figs. It was the smell of
chlorine and suntan lotion at the pool. It was the smell
in the bathroom of Clearasil and aftershave when
your brother began to shave. The grass in the summer
was hot as steam, but cooler in the evening. In the
evening when fathers got home from work or brothers
from summer jobs, there was the sound of the lawn
mower choking then revving then whirring across the
lawn. Then there was the smell then the same sound
at somebody else's then somebody else's house. The
fathers wore baseball caps and shirts; the brothers
went shirtless and you could see their shoulder and
arm muscles move and the zits on their backs. Tina
and Tammy wanted to stop and get off our bikes and
talk to them—Lydia and the boys and I did not.

The summer is sweet until you meet someone or find
something you maybe think is love and lose or throw

or give away whatever sense of you you have been starting to imagine. Something has started inside of you, inside your skin, and you want to do things you don't want but then you do. You want to go off alone or with somebody, not just anybody, else. You'd love for this person to look at you but you would be more frightened if they did. Will they? Why won't they look at you? What's wrong with you? Can everybody see?

Everyone else knows how to look. You don't.

One summer there was a giant storm. They had warned us about it so we had gone for candles and food and batteries. We'd meant to get back before it got bad but it started before they had thought. I remember not being able to see out the windshield and my mother driving through puddles that came up to the middle of the car door yelling "No brakes! No brakes!" as if anyone could hear. When we got home the yard was like a pond. The banks of the river had overflowed and lawn chairs and barbecues and garbage cans were floating. The dog that had followed me home was soaking and shivering on the porch and my mother said, yes, it could come inside, but only for the storm. We got in the house and put paper and rugs by the door to keep the water out but it didn't get that high, although almost.

The next day the streets were muddy and stank and everything was creepily, weirdly still. No one got that much damage, but we had been warned.

But nobody warns about everything.

Was that the same summer that Kenneth and Lydia stopped coming down for vacation? Their father moved somewhere and then there were no more bikes. Everyone was too cool or embarrassed to ride. We stayed in our rooms alone or with our dog to read or write in our diary. Neither Tina nor Tammy stayed in all the way through high school. One of them married her boyfriend; the other, I think, had her baby just by herself.

I wrote about things in my diary. I didn't write secrets, exactly, but kind of did. I wrote some in regular words but other things I wrote in only initials. Sometimes I even would change the initials so they were not the person's real ones. As in, instead of the initials of her name, I'd put SS for, like, someone in social studies class.

Later I started to make more things up. Not just initials, but also what didn't happen. I would invent. Sometimes I would write pretend letters, like what I would say if I went away and discovered you loved me too and how we would write letters as long as we had to because we just would. I wrote some of what I wouldn't say. I kept the diaries in a secret place.

In 1967, the year "The Door into Summer" was released, I was 11. I loved the Monkees' music but I did not love not knowing how to act when girls in my class got *Tiger Beat* magazine not to read about how they wrote their songs but to look at the pictures of who they thought was cutest, Micky or Davy. I had weird ideas in my head and pictures of things I did not understand. I had feelings like dark and light and felt like someone was watching me or that they weren't but I wanted them to. I tried to imagine who they were or what they looked like or that they said things to me. I remember one time seeing two white doves and wanting and hoping, pretending even, they meant something—a sign!—but knowing they didn't. I felt embarrassed about this and lonely about what I wanted; I did not tell. My older siblings, who were listening to Janis Joplin by then, and Big Brother and the Holding Company, would remember that time as the Summer of Love. They knew people who drove all the way to Haight-Ashbury. I did not want to be a hippie but I did want to be something I didn't know and I wanted to go someplace I did not know either.

By the time William Blake was 11, he had seen visions: One time God was nicely looking into a window of their house—one time a bunch of shining angels were singing in a tree. When Blake told his father about what he'd seen, his father beat him and told him not to make up lies. Blake learned about who to keep silent around and what to not talk about.

Here is a poem, "Song," from his first book, *Poetical Sketches,* which Blake wrote when he was 14:

How sweet I roam'd from field to field,
*   And tasted all the summer's pride,*
'Till I the prince of love beheld,
*   Who in the sunny beams did glide!*

He shew'd me lilies for my hair,
*   And blushing roses for my brow;*
He led me through his gardens fair,
*   Where all his golden pleasures grow.*

With sweet May dews my wings were wet,
*   And Phoebus fir'd my vocal rage;*
He caught me in his silken net,
*   And shut me in his golden cage.*

He loves to sit and hear me sing,
*   Then, laughing, sports and plays with me;*

> *Then stretches out my golden wing,*
>   *And mocks my loss of liberty.*

I bet he was starting to shave by then. A strange boy who had seen weird things and started to feel weird things in his body. They were sweet blush-making summery growing things that also could entrap you. You need to be careful whom you tell and if and how you tell them. He started to write poetry and paint and got himself apprenticed to an engraver.

Another of Blake's poems, "To Summer," from *Poetical Sketches*, begins like this:

> *O Thou who passest thro' our vallies in*
> *Thy strength, curb thy fierce steeds, allay the heat*
> *That flames from their large nostrils! thou,*
>   *O Summer,*
> *Oft pitched'st here thy golden tent, and oft*
> *Beneath our oaks hast slept, while we beheld*
> *With joy, thy ruddy limbs and flourishing hair.*

The word "steed," which is Poetry for "horse," is etymologically related to the word "stud." Blake's summer steed has sweat-messed hair and ruddy—red—skin like what one gets when one has exerted oneself with work or play or sex. His isn't a little toy plastic horse girls play with when they're young, but a giant panting fire-breathing animal.

Blake fell in love deeply and passionately, possessed by the wants of his body and heart, and when he was rejected he became despondent. One time after such a rejection, he met Catherine Boucher, who, though illiterate, knew exactly how to read him. She believed he was suffering and pitied him. Their courtship was short—they married soon and stayed married all their lives. He taught her to read, she helped him to paint and print his work. The last thing he ever drew, on his deathbed, was a sketch of Catherine to whom he said, "You have ever been an angel to me." They sunbathed together in the nude (not common in 18th-century London) in their back garden. One time when a friend out for a summer walk dropped by their home unexpectedly, Blake answered the door in his birthday suit and explained to the dumbfounded visitor that he'd interrupted Blake and Catherine playing Adam and Eve in the garden.

When Denise Levertov moved to Seattle in 1989, the summer felt good to her. In her late 60s and mostly retired from teaching, she found a house near Lake Washington with a view of Mount Rainier and began to write what would be her final poems. In "Settling" from *Evening Train* (1992), Levertov writes of the "clear gold of late summer," in which an eagle suns itself on a tree while Mount Rainier shines out.

Late summer is the best season in Seattle for exactly the things Levertov notices. Levertov thought about seasons and cyclical time, and also in her later years, after being received into the Roman Catholic Church, about long-term time and the time viewed through the lens of the Christian year, a cycle of dark and light, reckoning and anticipation, birth and death and rebirth and eternity. She saw the light of summer as a thing that moves and illuminates impermanent things like branches and sound and air—but also that remains before and after the things that it affects.

Levertov suggested a different view of the passing and long-lastingness of things when she wrote "Living" in an earlier book, *Summer Poems/1969,* in which each summer, each day, each minute seems the last.

The summer is knowing that nothing you sense, no matter its beauty or seeming longevity, will last.

I lie half asleep on the porch out back with the cats. I have sort of been reading but sort of not. I'm lying with a book facedown on my lap pretending I'm going to pick it back up and read. I hear clicking sounds and open my eyes. It's blurry at first but when I blink I see a hummingbird. We get them around here a lot in the summer. They come to the feeder we've set out for them. Sometimes I've seen four of them at a time on it, dipping their needle-y beaks in it and lifting their heads up and drinking. If I sit out here very still for a while, sometimes one of them will come flutter up close to me and I can hear its wings. They're like little motors. Their necks and the front of them shines and I don't want to move and I don't want this moment to end.

In the United States summer ends with Labor Day, our government having declared in 1894 a national holiday to celebrate the contributions made by laborers, workers, and unions to the welfare of the country. But nowadays unions are dying, and most of us, if we have a job, would love to not go back to work.

We get kind of manic with summer "fun," because we're aware it won't last. We do stuff impulsively, carelessly. At Seattle's Harborview hospital, emergency room visits increase by about 20 percent in the summer. People injure themselves more often in the summer with lawn mowers, garden tools, barbecues, grills. People poke out their eyes with power tools or get burned by fireworks or fire or the sun.

The dog we let in when the storm arrived was pregnant. She had her puppies in what had been my father's chair before he left. Some of them survived.

Fall

Fall

FALL IS EXCITING when you are a child. You're nervous but eager and also a little afraid. You get a new box of Crayolas or store-brand crayons. The tops are sharp and the bottoms are round and the papers around them are not furry yet. By the end of the year they'll be broken and rubbed and the sides of your hands will be blue and your desk will have marks that you've tried to rub off with your wet spitty fingers but can't.

Your mother has bought you some skirts and a couple of shirts and, some years, a pair of shoes. One time when my father came home he looked at my shoes and said, "For God's sake," then brought out his kit and taught me to polish them "decently." After that when we thought he was coming home, I'd polish my scruffy shoes until they shone.

You don't notice a lot when you're a child. This helps you remain a child. Stay innocent. You don't see how the world or you is changed. Sometimes when you're a child the time does not appear to pass. But it does.

Summer is pimples and sour sweat and girls in bikinis at the city pool with their not-quite-ready-to-shave and acne-shouldered boyfriends putting lotion on their backs. Summer is half of everyone half undressed and all of them better than you.

So after that, in fall, you cover up. Your mother no longer buys your clothes so now you can cover up differently. One day in eighth grade I wore a pair of midnight-purple corduroy pants and a long-sleeved top made of T-shirt material that had on it an appliqué of Saturn. The planet was almost the same dark purple as my pants. The rings around it were pink and chartreuse, my older sister, a hippie by then, having bought it for me at a brand-new store called a "head shop." I was kicked out of school and not allowed back until I agreed not to break the dress code again.

You want to appear like who you like. You don't want to look like you do. But the world around you changes, the time gets out of whack and you start looking wrong. Others around you are faster than you. You try to keep up but you can't. You walk around awkward and dull and feeling fake, and never know what to do with your stupid hands. You want to be like the ones you like and not have anything wrong with you and no one to think there is but something is.

The year after high school I got a scholarship to go to a school in England. I got there in September. The skies were like steel but misty and soft, and the sidewalks were wet in the morning. They'd told me I would be homesick but I was not. Then late in the morning the mist burned off and the trees shone slick with rusty-red and bright-yellow leaves and I was happy.

That fall I left home I fell in love. I remember her standing in the hall, her dark hair and her pale skin, the light pouring over her shoulders and hair that came from the window behind her. The shadows were long and the sun was low and the light was like honey and gold. I waited because I needed to (she was older than I and I knew how to wait) and then when we could we did what was meant to do. I remember a room and a cottage and walks and poring and poring and saying and not saying what. A long time after she wrote me a letter in which she tried to explain. She said I had unmoored her. I'd "blown into [her] life like 'the Wild West Wind.'"

I had to look it up.

This is the start of "Ode to the West Wind" by Percy Shelley:

> O *wild West Wind, thou breath of Autumn's being,*
> *Thou, from whose unseen presence the leaves dead*
> *Are driven, like ghosts from an enchanter fleeing…*

He wrote this in Florence, which I know because in the years since meeting that woman, I'd become somewhat obsessed with Shelley. He wrote it when he was living there, where I, in my early 30s, went to live too. On the morning of October 25, 1819, while walking alone in the Cascine woods on the banks of the Arno River, Shelley was caught in a storm. He and his young wife Mary (née Wollstonecraft Godwin) had been through a time of trouble.

They had had babies that lived or died, and she'd had a few miscarriages. He'd lost an ex-wife to suicide, she'd lost a half-sister to suicide, and Mary had written *Frankenstein*. ("It was on a dreary night in November, that I beheld the accomplishment of my toils. With an anxiety that almost amounted to agony..." Victor Frankenstein recalls of the moment he brought his poor monster to life.) Percy had gotten some vicious reviews and wondered if his work would ever be read the way he wanted. The storm and change of the season gave him an image of loss and redemption. The poem ends with a question: "If Winter comes, can Spring be far behind?"

I went to the Arno on October 25, 170 years to the day after Percy Shelley's storm. I stood on the bank in the quiet and warmth and said to myself some of what he had written. And then I sat down to wait.

Fall is also a season when someone can fall out of love. It's gradual and sad, or wild and thrashing, but always a beginning of an end. Was it something you did? A way you became disappointing? Or were you just stupid to think someone could love you? Did someone who once considered you novel get bored? Had they been mistaken to think you were worthy of love? Were you a fool to hope you maybe were? What's wrong with you? Or how can one not love the way one did?

What did you mean when you said, "I love you"? Why did you tell the things you did? But someone falls out, so you must too, or act as if you have, like everything's fine, you're fine, as if you are no longer a child or think like one or think or hope you could prevent or undo what has changed. Inside you are broken and partly dead, but you can't die just yet. You have to pretend you're fine. You have—even you—your pride.

Pride goeth before the fall like Adam did, and Eve, and also, I think in my pathetic, excusing, stupid way, the snake. They tried to know something they shouldn't know, do more than they knew how to do. They tried despite all the things they were told, they wanted to know too much. It goeth before the rest of us too, us misconceived and miserable, miscarried, poor, aborted, lonely, self-devouring selves. You know you've been given a gift—a life—but what are you doing with it? How will you carry on when you've been so wrong? It's damp and decaying outside, a mess, and you're out in the mess of it. While inside you are hollow, dry. Your mouth is dry, it's getting tight, you do not want to think the way you think. You try to go back, undo the fall, forget the falling out. Perhaps the way you felt was wrong. Perhaps how you remember isn't right.

In Florence I also used to go to the Brancacci Chapel to see the frescoes. The Church of Santa Maria del Carmine was going through restoration then, so scaffolding and white cloth covered everything, but I went there and looked and waited. I waited and waited and looked, and sometimes, if there was a breeze, a part of the cloth would lift and I would, through a shift or slit or billow, sort of, see. I remember sort of seeing though I do not remember what I saw.

But in a book I have at home, I looked it up.

Masaccio shows the story of The Fall. In *The Expulsion from the Garden of Eden*, Adam and Eve cower. Adam's shoulders stoop and the back of his bent-over neck is dark. He's covered his eyes with his hands and though his mouth is slightly open, he is quiet. Or maybe his voice is just so small that nobody else can hear him. He's ashamed. Eve is looking somewhere halfway up. Her right arm covers her naked chest, her crying mouth is open as a hole. She's crying—not tears—but crying like moaning, agonized, like, "God, what have we done?" Their innocence—like children's—has been lost. An angel dressed in red is hovering above them and wielding a sword as black as a blackened heart. The angel points away as if to say, "Get out." They're banished from Paradise. They are what they used to be no more. They know now, though they don't even know half, their lives will be full of suffering and they'll die.

If you look up "Fall, The" in *The New Dictionary of Theology*, published in 1987, the entry on page 386 reads, in its entirety: "See Original Sin."

The Gnostics imagined it differently—Adam and Eve, by eating the forbidden fruit of the Tree of Knowledge and thereby gaining the knowledge of evil and good, did not commit sin in disobedience to God, but were released from the jealous demiurge who'd created them but didn't want them to know the stuff he did.

I never saw it all at once, but just in little glimpses. I cannot imagine it differently.

Fail is fall except for the added I.

☙

Things fall apart; the centre cannot hold;
Mere anarchy is loosed upon the world,
The blood-dimmed tide is loosed, and everywhere
The ceremony of innocence is drowned

Yeats wrote "The Second Coming" in 1919, just after the end of World War I and after he'd lost his faith in the Irish Republican Brotherhood's attempts to peaceably create an independent Ireland. The war to end all wars had not ended war; the dream of returning to a traditional Irish past had proven, if not impossible, naive. The state of before can't be restored—all things fall apart in time. When blood is let it can't un-let. The fallen have fallen finally—they're dead.

"*The darkness drops again...*" the poem goes on. Yeats believed that history repeats itself in cycles. "*And what rough beast,*" he asks at the end of the poem, "*its hour come round at last, Slouches towards Bethlehem to be born?*"

History cycles in gyres like the seasons of the year. After the darkness falls there comes a time to rest. Then after a time something else begins, an innocent or Jesus, or a rough and slouching beast. Then there is a spring and light again, then fall, then dark again, again, again.

September is the ninth month of the year, but the syllable "sept" means seven (from Latin: *septem*). It used to be the seventh month in the 10-month Roman calendar; *octo, novem, decem* (8, 9, 10) were the rest. We kept those names when we switched to the 12-month Julian then Gregorian calendar. The names of these months go back to another time and another way to measure it. The words are the same but now mean something different.

In September the calendar goes out of whack. In fall, we set clocks back to save the day—light is getting scarce. Outside is the smell of decay and dirt. Evenings are cool but nights turn cold. You curl up as small as when you were a child and try not to think of your body.

In 1976, Neil Young made *Decade,* a 10-year retrospective triple disc. He was just in his early 30s but had already been looking back wearily for years. His fourth album, *Harvest* (1972), begins with the narrator thinking he'll "pack it in..." He wonders what he has accomplished so far, and how much he has left to do. There's a hangman character who says it's time to die. Young had lost friends to drugs, and tells an old man he feels a lot like him. Already Young felt old. So he took up with country musicians and bought a ranch, lived there with a woman and had a son and started to see up close and slow the passing of seasons.

Before it was called autumn, some Europeans called this season "harvest." This was the season of gathering, of seeing the yield of your work and saving up for the winter. You harvest crops with a sickle or scythe like you've seen in the old paintings and woodcuts of "The Grim Reaper," the harvester of souls. November 1st is All Saints' Day, then comes All Souls' Day, or the

Day of the Dead. They follow Hallowe'en, the holiday most looked forward to by children and queers. The word comes from "hallow," for holy, and evening. You dress up like something dead, a ghost or a ghoul or a skeleton, or a half-dead thing like a vampire or zombie or body snatcher, or something that never really lived—a character from a cartoon, a hero, a goddess, a doll. You make bigger or smaller a part of yourself, or show a hidden part—a man becomes a woman, a woman a god, a child somebody permanent and strong.

You go to the graveyard on All Souls' Day. You try to pretend the fallen can come back. You try to pretend they do, if only for a single day or night. Because you would give anything for just one day, for just one night or word or look or hand. To have them back with you, you would give anything. You would give up your life.

In better years you'll celebrate, remember and be grateful that you knew them though if only for a time.

On the hallowed holy night between All Saints' and

All Souls' Days, the veil between the worlds gets thin. You can believe, one time a year, that someone you once loved could be alive again.

You cannot, though, believe that way for long.

A few years ago my artist friend Noah Saterstrom and I made a Day of the Dead altar together for an exhibit in a library in Tucson. He painted a picture of a woman and children, and in front of the altar-like thing was a screen you could almost see through. We put things of ours on the altar and made crepe-paper flowers and invited other people to too. The back of the altar was chalkboards I wrote some sentences for. They said things like: What did he leave you with? and What did she take? and What are you waiting for now? What can you not remember? Can you forget? What will you do? What do you wish you'd done? And people wrote answers and other questions on pieces of paper and slipped them behind the screen like we were leaving them for the dead. It was sort of like writing Santa letters except everybody knew. But everyone also wanted to act, for a while at least, like the words and things we left for the dead would get to them. Like maybe they would know. People left things privately, quietly, made pictures or wrote little words and tucked them in. We did this throughout our allotted time, then at the end of the exhibit season, returned the flowers and things to people who had left them. We couldn't pretend they'd gone somewhere they hadn't.

Whenever I find myself growing grim about the mouth; whenever it is a damp, drizzly November in my soul; whenever I find myself involuntarily pausing before coffin warehouses, and bringing up the rear of every funeral I meet; and especially whenever my hypos get such an upper hand of me... then I account it high time to get to sea as soon as I can.

That's Ishmael, near the beginning of *Moby-Dick*.

He's feeling like a dying, if not quite dead yet, soul. When Melville was writing, "hypos" referred to what we would now call "depression." Some writers go through this from time to time. Some people say it's seasonal. It's nice to think it's limited to that.

Sometimes Melville was dull or weird or volatile, but also sometimes he escaped by going to the sea. Then when he came back he wrote what became successful adventure books (*Omoo, Typee*, etc.). In 1850, he was finishing another novel that he described to an acquaintance as

> *a romance of adventure, founded upon certain wild legends of the Southern Sperm Whale Fisheries, and illustrated by the author's own personal experience, of two years & more, as a harpooner...*

Then he read Nathaniel Hawthorne. Here's some of what Melville wrote in an August 1850 review of Hawthorne's *Mosses from an Old Manse:*

> *For spite of all the Indian-summer sunlight on the hither side of Hawthorne's soul, the other side—like the dark half of the physical sphere—is shrouded in a blackness, ten times black... You may be witched by his sunlight,—transported by the bright gildings in the skies he builds over you;—but there is the blackness of darkness beyond; and even his bright gildings but fringe, and play upon the edges of thunder-clouds...*

Then later: "It is that blackness in Hawthorne, of which I have spoken, that so fixes and fascinates me."

Melville was 31 that year and Hawthorne was 46. The younger was "fixed" by the elder's "blackness," and then, when he met him, all of him.

My *New Oxford American Dictionary* defines "Indian summer" as "a period of unusually dry, warm weather occurring in late autumn." A season has left, but then it comes back like a hiccup. It jars you and reminds you what is missing. The sun on the side of the soul, Melville thought, was paired with a dark, concealed side. Hawthorne showed Melville, or so he thought, his own dark soul, and also that a writer could actually write it. That fall, when they met, they took long walks and talked for hours, and wrote each other letters. In one of his letters to Hawthorne, Melville says: "The divine magnet is on you, and my magnet responds." A later one rhapsodizes:

> *Whence come you, Hawthorne? By what right do you drink from my flagon of life? And when I put it to my lips—lo, they are yours and not mine. I feel that the Godhead is broken up like the bread at the Supper, and that we are the pieces. Hence this infinite fraternity of feeling... when the big hearts strike together, the concussion is a little stunning.*

Melville, the way one writer can for another, fell in love. This is the state in which he rewrote the harpooner adventure into the massive, great, Romantic *Moby-Dick*.

I don't know exactly why Melville thought of Hawthorne's soul as having an "Indian summer," but no one really agrees about exactly where the phrase came from. Some people think that "Indians" first described the seasonal phenomenon to Europeans, others that Europeans first noticed it occurred where "Indians" lived, others that it most often occurred when trade ships arrived from India. But I learned this phrase as an echo of the offensive phrase "Indian giver," which meant someone you couldn't trust because when they gave you a gift, they later wanted it back. The hiccup of "Indian summer" is seen as a tease, a cheat, a gift that is not a gift. You might think that way if you don't understand the kind of circular economy or culture of reciprocity described in Lewis Hyde's *The Gift*. There he explains that when you're given something, you want to give something back. Your wealth is not about what you have or can get or get away with. Rather, it is about doing something good for someone else, passing a blessing around to make it more. What you have isn't only yours but others' too.

"Indian Summer," from Beat Happening's 1988 *Jamboree* (K Records), and the best twee-indie song of the late 1980s, begins, like All Souls' Day, in a cemetery. It's by Heather Lewis, Calvin Johnson, and Bret Lunsford. It's about when your childhood is almost over but you still have a kind of innocence as an adult. It says nice stuff about growing up and not wanting yet to forget. It starts in a cemetery, with kids eating wild fruit and riding motorbikes, exploring sex and hoping they and these wild days will never end, that they will never change.

But of course people change. Like cherries and apples, we are seasonal. Then after they're ripe the bushes and trees they grow on are stripped down for the winter. One time in your life a cemetery can be a place for a picnic date. Another time it turns into a place you pray you will not have to visit very often. One time in your life having sex is being a cheerful, hungry kid at a picnic feast. But when a part of you or someone you are trying to love has been messed up by memory or loss or grief then you cannot be a kid like that again.

When I was 40, my parents died. My mom died first then one month later my father. A month after that, I had a "commitment ceremony" with the love of my life who is now my legally married wife. The same year I published a book, *The End of Youth*. If you're lucky your parents will die before you, as is the natural order. If they are unlucky, you'll die before them, and they will remember for the rest of their lives their child who died.

It was right before the fall—in August—when my mother was diagnosed with stage 3 colon cancer. I quit my job and went to care for her. We didn't have any old business by then and were grateful to be with each other. She died six months later, in January. My father died very suddenly the following month of a heart attack or stroke (we were not ever sure). He'd listened to Frank Sinatra some and I think kind of thought of himself as somewhat like him—a man who held court, who could tell a good tale and always looked good in a suit. A drinker, a smoker of one pack a day, a serial spouse who didn't put up with what he called female "nonsense."

When Frank Sinatra turned 50, he wore a hat all the time in public because he was going bald. In 1965, after already having had a successful career, he and his sometime arranger-conductor Gordon Jenkins, who was also in his 50s, decided to make an album of songs they thought of as "self-remembrances." It's called *September of My Years.*

The first song of the album—written by Jimmy Van Heusen and Sammy Cahn—begins in the summer, but the seasons pass so quickly the singer keeps hankering back for his youth.

A lot of places on the album refer to being in the "autumn" of life. I find this word more honest than "middle age." When you get to your 40s or 50s, you're not in the "middle" of your life; you're past it. Whereas in autumn, the year is three-quarters over and it's time to gather, and if you don't what's left will rot. The winter is coming, you're slowing down and looking back. You think either "It Was a Very Good Year" (the fourth song on *September of My Years,* written by Ervin Drake) or that it wasn't and there is not much good to store up for the cold.

Though it would have fit in, Sinatra did not include "Autumn Leaves" on this album. That perfectly September song, with English lyrics by Johnny Mercer after the French "Les feuilles mortes" by Jacques Prevert and Joseph Kosma, equates this season of physical decay with the end of a love affair. The days grow long and lonely.

Sinatra had sung it on a previous album, *Where Are You?* (1957). Perhaps, with Elvis's ascent, Sinatra was already thinking his days were numbered. Perhaps, like Young, he felt prematurely old.

Actually, I'm only guessing that my father thought of himself like Frank Sinatra. I do not know because I never asked him. Maybe I never asked because when he was in his cups, he sometimes got belligerent. Or maybe I took it too much to heart that I should be seen, not heard. Or maybe I never asked because I decided early on to act like I cared even less than he.

But I have also never, before I was thinking about this stuff this week, asked myself why I didn't ask. I never asked my father what he remembered about his youth. Or what he remembered about being a brother or son, or what he did in "the war," or how it was to come back and why the navy made him leave. I never asked my father why he left.

Another song on the Sinatra album—"It Gets Lonely Early," by Jimmy Van Heusen and Sammy Cahn— talked about the sadness of being alone after your children have left home.

My mother died in her 60s and my father at 73. Sinatra lived till his early 80s. Neil Young is still alive. My wife is now three years younger than the age my mom was when she died.

As I'm writing this, I'll soon be 64. As in the Beatles' song, which when it first came out, seemed impossibly far off in the future—an age I would never be. And, in truth, for a few years a lot of years ago, I didn't expect I'd live this long. But now that I have, I am grateful.

Not only grateful that I am still alive and have the life I do, but also for even the things I regret.

The older you get, the more people near you die. If you're lucky you see it coming and can prepare or make amends and be with them. You can remember with them and be glad. You can tell them "I love you" and "Good-bye."

But if you can't remember, if you cannot look back at the very good years or bad ones, it's like there is nothing to harvest. It's like whatever you did was never done. It's like part of the person you were is already dead. If you can no longer remember yourself, then who is there to know?

I saw my friend Tom the other week, and he asked about our mutual friend and I told him her mother had died. "It ended quick," I said, "a heart attack," and Tom said, "Oh." Then he paused and said, "That was lucky." Then he looked at me a second and said, and he sounded ashamed when he did, "I kind of wish that would happen to my dad." Tom's dad, like our friend's mother, has Alzheimer's. Alzheimer's can go on a long, long time and Tom's father keeps getting worse. He's getting lost all the time these days, forgetting not only recent stuff, but old things and confusing them and always forgetting more. "He's scared a lot too," Tom said. He looked scared too.

There's a "care home community" in Arlington, Texas, the last place I lived with my parents, "specifically designed to deliver…unsurpassed care to seniors with memory impairment." I think this means it's for people with things like Alzheimer's, people who can't take care of themselves because they can't remember things. You do not know how to care for them and can't bear to see them not be who they were. At least, you remind yourself, they got to get old. They had, whether they remember or not, a life. You try to remember for them.

The name of this care home community is Autumn Leaves. I think that's a reference to both the song and the season of leaving.

You look back and think about what you did and what you neglected to do. You fall back on excuses: "If only..." "If I..." You're happy or grateful or sad you don't forget. You miss who is dead and you fear for the next to die. You, selfishly, want to have no more grief, but you know you will unless you're the one who dies next. The fall is you trying to live how you are, not spending too much time remembering, but neither afraid of how little is left. You have learned now, despite what always has been since you were a child, there will come a winter that will not be followed by spring.

�֍

Winter

Winter

IT'S DARK OUTSIDE so winter inside makes sense. It's cold so you cover up. It's stuffy and sweaty inside your clothes but your fingers and face are freezing. The sky is gray and the trees are leafless, they've given up, and if there's a sun it's very hard to see. The nights are long, they last forever, until you're supposed to get up and then you can't. You don't want to get out of bed or see or talk to anyone. You want to sleep and not wake up. You want to burrow. Things are supposed to get "better" in spring but that isn't what you want. The winter trees have given up so why can't you?

Animals thicken their coats and put on fat. They curl up tight, sometimes alone but sometimes with another or a group. Some sleep throughout the winter—others wake up, sort of, sometimes. Bears, chipmunks, hedgehogs, porcupines, and squirrels all get to hibernate. But also some cold-blooded things like snakes. Some kinds of snakes sleep months in mobs like giant tangled twitchy balls of string. Some insects hibernate, including bees. In some hives, the worker bees die and the only one who wakes again is the queen. Birds fly south. You burrow in caves or under rocks or deep in rooms with books and blankets and you barely move.

You move as slow as sludge.

The word "winter" comes from Old English and Germanic roots related to *waeter,* or water. In the northern hemisphere it's the season of rain and snow. Officially, it starts on the winter solstice, the shortest and darkest day of the year (December 21 or 22), when where you live is tipping away from the sun. It ends on the vernal equinox (March 21 or 22), when the days and nights, the dark and light, are getting back in balance.

By winter the crops have been brought in and with less work to do outside, and awful, awful weather, your northern ancestors stayed inside a lot. They sat by the fire for light and heat. Some people found this cozy but some others suffered from, and so made others suffer, cabin fever. As if they were inside so much, their insides started to fester.

To pass the time they told each other stories.

In the kids' book *While the Bear Sleeps* (by Caitlin Matthews, illustrated by Judith Christine Wells, 1999), a girl is outside when the first snow starts. She seeks refuge in a cave that turns out to be a bear's den. But the big, hairy bear is nice and tells her she can stay with him in the cave and sleep because winter is the time "to look inside yourself and remember important things."

But sometimes you do too much of that.

A line in Shakespeare's *The Winter's Tale* says "A sad tale's best for winter." Sometimes in winter being sad is all you think about.

Seasonal affective disorder, or SAD, I read on the Mayo Clinic webpage,

> *is a type of depression that's related to changes in seasons... If you're like most people with SAD, your symptoms start in the fall and continue into the winter months, sapping your energy and making you feel moody.*

In fall you start to fall apart—in winter you're already fallen. It happens again like it always does which you should know by now but you do not. Or you do know but stupidly you pretend you don't. You try to sleep to get away from being alive and suffering. You try to sleep to undo what your passion turns you to. Your passion comes from somewhere both inside of you and outside where you do not understand, or if you do, or think you do, you fear it as much as you desire it—it is mysterious.

"Passion" is when you are not just alive, not just breathing and eating and crapping and sleeping and not really caring whether you wake up or not. Passion is being alive a lot. You want to wake up, you want to want. You want to move toward and do something. Maybe you know a reason or maybe you don't but nothing stops you. You want and desire and yearn toward a person or people or an idea or something.

But passion, the word, derives from the Latin *passio*, which means to suffer. To want means you will suffer. To want is to know you might but might not have. You'll have but then you will have not, you'll lose. To open the heart means it will break. You do not want to not want. You have to hope you will get through the bad, the worst, and that you will, or someone else will, come out, living, on the other side.

"Don't brush off that yearly feeling as simply a case of the 'winter blues' or a seasonal funk that you have to tough out on your own," the Mayo Clinic website goes on to say. "Take steps to keep your mood and motivation steady throughout the year."

It's amazing how unhelpful some websites can be.

One time many years ago, when I was in a state, I told my friends I was going out of town but I was lying. Instead I stayed at home in bed alone. I pulled down the blinds and shut off the phone and turned out the lights and curled up beneath the blankets and sort of slept. It was the closest I could get to not existing. I couldn't imagine waking up. I also didn't want to but I guess sometimes I did.

That winter I went camping by myself. I climbed up a mountain and walked around. It was snowy and gray and cold but I didn't really feel that until I got lost. Then, when it began to seem like I really might truly not get back, that's when I wanted to. Somehow, though I do not know how, I found a trail then got back to my tent.

I remember the next morning waking up and looking out the tent flap and seeing as if suddenly the normal day looked beautiful.

I knew that I was still alive and suddenly felt grateful.

"The Snow Queen" is Hans Christian Andersen's tale about a boy who falls in love and can't escape. She's beautiful, chilly, white as snow, and when she whooshes by him in a sleigh, she dazzles him. He ties his sled to hers and she pulls him around and he feels great like he has never felt before. Then he starts to freeze.

Hypothermia is caused by getting cold. Your temperature drops, your body slows, your metabolism shifts. You shiver, your breathing and heart rates race. Your mind begins to blur and sometimes even—you cannot help yourself—you tear off your clothes. The Snow Queen tells the boy to come inside her coat. When he is all wrapped up in her, she kisses him. But inside her coat, it's colder than he expected, his heart starts to freeze, he feels like he's dying. The Snow Queen stops embracing him before she kisses him to death.

He wants her to kiss him again but now he's afraid. It's like his body is not his own anymore. She takes him to her palace and he stays with her for what feels like forever. At night he looks up at the dark winter sky. In the day he sleeps at her feet like a beaten dog.

The phone call came on a morning in December. They didn't say how it happened but the roads were icy and we knew he'd had to drive. My friend needed to come home, they said, and he asked me and so I went with him.

He and I went and we stayed with the baby and widow. The widow sat on the couch a lot. The baby needed to be held. One of us sat and held the widow's hand or answered the phone and listened. The other held the baby and cooed or followed behind it when it tried to walk. It walked around falling and looking and saying "Daddy?" Then after a while we'd switch and the other would sit with her and the other would take the baby. Everyone—his family, workmates, friends, his widow—was sad and very shocked.

This was still in the days of Walkmans and mine had only one CD in it when I'd thrown it in my bag, and when the baby or widow would sleep, one of us stayed inside with them and the other could go outside and if it was me I took a walk with the Walkman.

Outside it was frozen, the fields were stubbled with brown-white furrows and clods stuck up from the snow. The side of the highway had dirty lumps of ice from the slush the trucks threw off. The air was dry and the world seemed not alive. The only sounds were me, my breath, and walking, and in my ears and head the songs of Schubert's *Winterreise.*

The words of the song cycle, from poems by Wilhelm Müller, tell the story of a young man who falls in love with a girl in May; later, in winter, she rejects him and he becomes despondent. He tries to get over his despair by going away alone. His only companions on his winter journey include a crow, some dogs, the rain and snow, a river, and finally a poor, old hurdy-gurdy man.

Schubert started getting sick in his twenties with headaches, horrible skin, and hair loss (for a while he wore a wig). He knew these were signs of syphilis and suspected he wouldn't live long. Previously, he had premiered his songs in evening salons at his own place or the homes of friends, where everyone would eat and drink and sing together. But *Winterreise* happened differently. After Schubert's death, his friend, Josef von Spaun, remembered this:

> *For a time, Schubert's mood became gloomier and he seemed upset. When I asked him what the matter was, he merely said to me, "Come to Schober's today.*

> *I will sing you a cycle of awe-inspiring songs."* He
> *then, with a voice full of feeling, sang...* Winterreise
> *for us. We were quite dumbfounded by the gloomy*
> *mood of these songs.*

That evening at the home of poet and librettist Franz
von Schober, Schubert presented the first 12 of the 24
songs that eventually made up *Winterreise*. After that
evening at Schober's, though he continued to decline,
Schubert kept composing.

Von Spaun also remembered this:

> *On Nov 11 [1828] he had to take to his bed. Although*
> *dangerously ill, he felt no pain and complained*
> *only of weakness. Now and then he would fall into*
> *delirium, during which time he sang continuously.*
> *He used his few lucid intervals to revise the second*
> *part of* Winterreise... *On Nov 19, at 3 o'clock in the*
> *afternoon, he breathed his last.*

Schubert sang while dying. The Hasidim dance while
mourning. I learned recently from Donna Krolik

Hollenberg's excellent biography of Jewish-then-Catholic writer Denise Levertov that after Levertov learned that her father had risen "from his bed shortly before his death to dance the Hasidic dance of praise," Levertov wrote the poem "In Obedience." That's the one that includes the lines "Let my dance / be mourning then..."

Some people actually welcome death, and not because they've given up or are desperate to put themselves out of their misery. They welcome it as a natural phase, transition, or kind of graduation, from an earthly, bodily life toward some other form of living that is better. This might include an afterlife or some mysterious way of being where you'll get to see the ones you have loved who've died. Or one in which you get to be at peace. The people who believe this die in hope.

Midwinter festivals have been part of northern cultures, where the winters are extreme, forever. Many of them—Yule (pagan), Sadeh (Persian), Christmas

(Euro-Christian)—have in common a story of the return after darkness of light. In the Christianity I practice, Christmas is preceded by Advent (from Latin *adventus*; ad "to" + *venire* "come"), a period in which believers look forward to the arrival of the divine in the form of a baby. Expected and waited and hoped for. Yet when it arrives you can't quite believe but also you cannot imagine not.

The "it" that arrives for Christians at Christmas is Jesus, the baby that is a human-god, whose story ends with the Passion. That is his suffering, which is an end, but not an end, but really a beginning, again, of light in a season of dark.

There's a picture of my wife from before we were married. She's smiling in her winter coat. Her hair is not as gray as it is now. The day is bright. We're walking on a path beside a field. It's in the country and quiet the way it only gets in snow, and she is happy. I am happy too. I took the picture in England where we went the first Christmas we spent together. I took her there to see the people who sort of adopted me when I was a teenager.

It's great over there at Christmas. They eat good food like bite-sized raisin-apple pies and buttery potatoes. At night you sit inside where it's warm and laugh and tell the same stupid tales you've all told a million times but you are happy to hear them again.

You go out to let out the dog. Outside it's very cold and dark but also there is light from the moon and stars. The snow crunches under your feet and your cheeks get cold. The dog runs around and sniffs and when it comes back you go inside to the warmth and the light and your friends. Someone is changing the baby now and someone is making a sandwich and telling again for the millionth time a story. You stand inside the house of your friends and feel and see and everyone is in love and alive and you get to be here, grateful, too, however long, this time, the winter lasts.

Afterword

THE FOUR CHAPTERS of this book originally appeared as essays in Seattle's alternative weekly, *The Stranger*, between 2014 and 2016. They appeared in print before Trump was elected and everything changed. As if whatever good things had happened with Obama would be undone and you didn't know whether to cry or collapse or scream. It was a time to do something practical, like show up for the women's march and volunteer for reproductive rights and immigrants and racial justice and the environment. I found myself listening to students who wanted to quit reading and writing in order to work for whatever cause they felt they needed to. I couldn't blame them.

Plus, I was in my 60's and had been finding it increasingly difficult to write, hard sometimes to even want to write. Maybe I was just tired, but maybe something about me—my era, my style, my voice—was obsolete, and now it was time for other writers. Print media was dying, so why not me? At least metaphorically. Maybe I didn't have much to say any more.

Then in early 2021 Covid happened and everything changed again but also differently. The pandemic felt less like the guy in Munch's *The Scream* and more like the landscape behind him—with everything gray and yellow and morbid and over with. But then in the summer Black Lives Matter was everywhere and people were pushing back against the murders of George Floyd and how many others, and so in the midst of numbness and despair was a burst of aliveness.

Things I had given up on were coming around again.

Was this like a change of season?

Today, as I write this afterword, it's summer. It's hot and dry and windy and hot, and on my bad-mood days I worry that the summer, fall, winter, and spring seasons I love here in the northern part of the western hemisphere will turn into the seasons of drought, fire, storm, and flood.

I know that won't happen, right?

During the years I was writing about the seasons, I became very aware of cycles of life and death, despair and joy, of light coming after dark. The seasons gave me ways to think about humans in history and time. This gave me, sometimes, hope.

But when I found myself in personal or social periods of desolation, I forgot. Maybe like how in the winter it's hard to imagine spring, I forgot there was anything else besides despair. I needed—I need—to remember the seasons change. I need to remember the dark abates, that light and life return.

This is a story I need to believe.

Ackowledgements

THESE ESSAYS WERE COMMISSIONED by Christopher Frizzelle, and first appeared in *The Stranger*. They would not exist without Frizzelle, the most thoughtful, insightful, and supportive editor a writer could ever hope for. This book is for him.

Thanks to Corianton Hale, Lesley Hazleton, and John Whitney, SJ for support along the way. Ya'll know how you helped!

Thanks to Chatwin Books: Phil Bevis for finding the right title, Vladimir Verano for the cover, Annie Brulé for interior design.

Thanks again and always to Christine Galloway, beloved for life.

REBECCA BROWN is the author of many books
published in the US and abroad. She lives in Seattle.